Mx

and

Mx

summersdale

MX AND MX

Copyright © Summersdale Publishers Ltd, 2022

Compiled by Samuel Alexander

An Hachette UK Company
www.hachette.co.uk

Summersdale Publishers Ltd
Part of Octopus Publishing Group Limited
Carmelite House
50 Victoria Embankment
LONDON
EC4Y 0DZ
UK

www.summersdale.com

Printed and bound in China

ISBN: 978-1-80007-553-5

Substantial discounts on bulk quantities of Summersdale books are available to corporations, professional associations and other organizations. For details contact general enquiries: telephone: +44 (0) 1243 771107 or email: enquiries@summersdale.com.

To...

From...

The most important thing in my heart is that I love you.

SARAH GAILEY

If we are
not here for
LOVE,
what are we
here for?

JUNO DAWSON

FROM THE
MOMENT
WE STARTED
TALKING, I
KNEW THAT
I WANTED
YOU AROUND
FOREVER

NEVER FORGET,
DEAR ONE,
HOW DEEPLY I HAVE
loved you
ALL THESE YEARS.

RACHEL CARSON

You could have
had anything else
in the world, and
you asked for me.

CASSANDRA CLARE

Love isn't some scarce resource to battle over. Love can be infinite, as much as your heart can open.

XIRAN JAY ZHAO

I USED TO
THINK A LOVE
LIKE THIS WAS
IMPOSSIBLE TO
FIND — THEN
I MET YOU

LOVE
has no
boundaries.

ANDREJA PEJIĆ

I am that clumsy human, always loving, loving, loving. And loving.

FRIDA KAHLO

OUR LOVE IS TOO BIG TO FIT IN A BOX

**But our story
is also a tale of
triumph, because
in the end love
conquered all.**

JÓHANNA SIGURÐARDÓTTIR

Love has
penetrated
my heart with
its flame,

And is ever
rekindled with
new warmth.

ALCUIN

BE WHO YOU
WANT TO BE;
I'LL STILL
ALWAYS
LOVE YOU

**IF YOU WERE HERE
I WOULD JUST**

AND FEEL BETTER.

IRIS MURDOCH

I'm a big proponent of all love winning.

JONATHAN van NESS

Love is
boundary-less.

ANGEL HAZE

YOU
ARE
MY
HOME

You had to be willing to fight in order for a love story to last a lifetime.

CRISTINA MARRERO

LOVE IS
the whole
thing.
We are only
pieces.

RUMI

Love can happen
between any
people, because
we're all human.

EDDIE IZZARD

There are a hundred paths through the world that are easier than loving. But, who wants easier?

MARY OLIVER

LOVE DOESN'T NEED TO BE PERFECT; IT JUST NEEDS TO BE TRUE

NO MATTER
WHAT ELSE,
WE HAVE
LOVE.

Always love.

P. C. CAST

YOU MAKE ME
HAPPY LIKE NO
ONE ELSE CAN

♥

When you
love someone,
you are sure.
You don't need
time to decide.

NINA LaCOUR

I love you without knowing how, or when, or from where.

I love you directly without problems or pride.

PABLO NERUDA

Love that
stammers, that
stutters, is apt
to be the love
that loves best.

GABRIELA MISTRAL

LOVED YOU THEN, LOVE YOU STILL; ALWAYS HAVE, ALWAYS WILL

We'll keep

EACH
OTHER

firmly on
this earth.

NINO CIPRI

Tenderness is greater proof of love than the most passionate of vows.

MARLENE DIETRICH

I WISH I COULD TURN BACK THE CLOCK — I'D FIND YOU SOONER AND LOVE YOU LONGER

Love is awesome and endless.

NEIL PATRICK HARRIS

Love is louder
than the pressure
to be perfect.

DEMI LOVATO

I FEEL I AM
in love with you,
AND IT SHOULD
BE SPRING.

PATRICIA HIGHSMITH

YOU ARE MY EVERYTHING

True love, the kind that lasts and survives for years, is always full of passion and craziness.

ABDELLAH TAÏA

To love is so startling it leaves little time for anything else.

EMILY DICKINSON

We are all
DESERVING
of love.

SANDRA BULLOCK

EVERY DAY WITH YOU IS THE BEST DAY OF MY LIFE

A line can be straight,
or a street, but the
human heart, oh, no,
it's curved like a road
through mountains.

TENNESSEE WILLIAMS

There is never a time or place for true love. It happens accidentally, in a heartbeat, in a single flashing, throbbing moment.

SARAH DESSEN

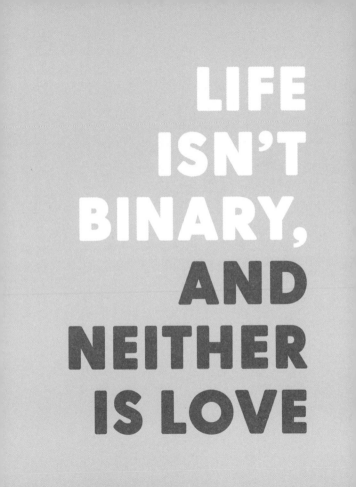

Every memory
of your face,
every cadence
of your voice
is joy.

MARGARET MEAD

YOU MAKE EVERY SINGLE DAY SOMETHING TO SEIZE AND CHERISH, AND YOU MAKE THE FUTURE *unshakably bright.*

SESSA COOKIE MUELLER

I'LL ALWAYS CHOOSE YOU

I think romance is anything honest. As long as it's honest, it's so disarming.

KRISTEN STEWART

What you need,
maybe all you
need, in fact, is the
willingness to love.

JENNIFER FINNEY BOYLAN

By doing the work
to love ourselves
more, I believe we
will love each
other better.

LAVERNE COX

THE HAPPIEST I'VE EVER FELT WAS THE MOMENT I LEARNED THAT YOU LOVED ME TOO

My plan is just
to love harder
than I've ever
loved before,
hide nothing.

SAM SMITH

LOVE IS A

wildfire

THAT CANNOT BE CONTAINED BY ANY MERE ELEMENT KNOWN TO MAN.

CRISTINA MARRERO

THEY SAY YOU
ONLY FALL IN
LOVE ONCE, BUT
EVERY TIME I
THINK OF YOU
I FALL IN LOVE
ALL OVER AGAIN

Other people
too have friends
that they love;

But ours was
a love such as
few friends
have known.

YUAN ZHEN

Whatever we had missed, we possessed together the precious, the incommunicable past.

WILLA CATHER

If there's anything worth any risk at all, it's got to be love, right?

JESSICA VERDI

I LOVE YOU
MORE THAN
WORDS CAN
EXPRESS

♥

To love someone
else enough to
forget about
yourself even
for one moment
is to be free.

JEANETTE WINTERSON

I am utterly
helpless,
I can only
LOVE YOU.

RADCLYFFE HALL

YOU MAKE ME THE BEST VERSION OF MYSELF

It's funny that
it's so plain that
it's love that
makes the world
go round.

IRIS MURDOCH

I'M AMAZED WHEN I LOOK AT YOU, BECAUSE EVERYTHING I'VE EVER WANTED IS RIGHT IN FRONT OF ME

I want to say it as many times as I want – I love you, I love you, I love you, I love you.

ADAM SILVERA

We can't be
anywhere
except
TOGETHER.

FRANCESCA LIA BLOCK

Love is the most
incredible gift to give
and to receive as
a human being.

ELLIOT PAGE

Love is the emblem of eternity; it confounds all notion of time; effaces all memory of a beginning, all fear of an end.

MADAME DE STAËL

All the laws on the statutes, all the courts in the universe, cannot tear it from the soil, once love has taken root.

EMMA GOLDMAN

IT WAS AN
ecstatic
TIME WHEN
WE FOUND
EACH OTHER.

JANE WAGNER

LOVE IS
SITTING BESIDE
SOMEONE,
DOING
NOTHING, AND
YET FEELING
PERFECTLY
HAPPY

To death
and back,
I love you.

HEATHER MATARAZZO

Love needs
no publicity
because

LOVE
JUST IS.

PRINCE

I NEED YOU
LIKE A HEART
NEEDS A BEAT

You have grown so much to be a part of my life that it is empty without you.

ELEANOR ROOSEVELT

I miss you even more than I could have believed; and I was prepared to miss you a good deal.

VITA SACKVILLE-WEST

I often think of
you and see you
in my dreams.

PYOTR ILYICH TCHAIKOVSKY

YOU WILL ALWAYS BE MY REASON TO BELIEVE IN THAT *soul-hugging* KIND OF LOVE.

KRISTEN KISH

I WANT TO WAKE UP NEXT TO YOU EVERY DAY

♥

Nothing ever
truly made sense
until you came
into my life.

MARIAH LINNEY

I feel like

LOVE IS

the thing
we were
created for.

NIECY NASH

I didn't want
to live a life
without love.

EDIE WINDSOR

TOGETHER IS MY FAVOURITE PLACE TO BE

Since I am bound
to you by love,
I wish you
to be mine.

MARSILIO FICINO

Once you follow
your heart, it's
all of a sudden
so easy.

STEPHANIE ALLYNNE

I LET YOU INTO MY WORLD, AND THEN YOU BECAME MY WORLD

For just as I have
been sure, as I
am now, and so
will I always be

That I am cherished
in your heart,
you in mine.

WALAFRID STRABO

Where there
is great love,
there are
always
MIRACLES.

WILLA CATHER

In your eyes
I see myself
become what I
always dreamed
I could be.

ISABEL MILLER

YOU WON A
PIECE OF MY
HEART THE
DAY WE MET;
NOW YOU
HAVE THE
WHOLE THING

AFTER ALL,
WHAT ARE WE DOING
ON EARTH,
WHAT ARE WE
LOOKING FOR?
TO BE HAPPY AND
to be loved!

ALICE NKOM

One is loved
because one is loved.
No reason is needed
for loving.

PAULO COELHO

Every moment is made glorious by the light of love.

RUMI

I think it is high
time to tell you
that I think of
you constantly.

MARLENE DIETRICH

WHEN I WANT
TO SMILE,
I KNOW
EXACTLY
WHAT TO DO:
I JUST CLOSE
MY EYES AND
THINK OF YOU

**HOW PRETTILY
WE SWIM.
NOT IN WATER,
NOT ON LAND,**
but in love.

GERTRUDE STEIN

Fear should not get in the way of how you love or who you love.

JANELLE MONÁE

EVERY TIME I SEE YOU, I'M MORE CONVINCED THAT WE BELONG TOGETHER

Your lips bring
blessings –
my beloved.

MARGARET MEAD

I ache
to hold you
CLOSE.

ELEANOR ROOSEVELT

Each time you
love, love as
deeply as if it
were forever.

AUDRE LORDE

I'LL ALWAYS WANT TO BE IN YOUR ARMS

You're my polar star.
I'll go wherever
you guide me.

XIRAN JAY ZHAO

Being deeply loved by someone gives you strength, while loving someone deeply gives you courage.

ANONYMOUS

I COULD
SPEND A
WHOLE DAY
WITH YOU
AND STILL
MISS YOU
THE SECOND
YOU LEFT

You are one
of my nicest
thoughts.

GEORGIA O'KEEFFE

SINCE I MET YOU I SMILE A LOT MORE OFTEN

I truly believe this, and for me, the basis of art is love.

DAVID HOCKNEY

You shall have
every smile and
every breath of
tenderness.

ANNE LISTER

MY LOVE
FOR YOU IS
LIMITLESS

The things we truly love stay with us always, locked in our hearts as long as life remains.

JOSEPHINE BAKER

I think of you
daily, and
am always
devotedly

YOURS.

OSCAR WILDE

Now I know
the meaning
of life is love.

CARA DELEVINGNE

I WANT EVERY TOMORROW TO BE WITH YOU

♥

PERHAPS WE WERE
FRIENDS FIRST AND
LOVERS SECOND.
BUT THEN PERHAPS

*this is what
lovers are.*

ANDRÉ ACIMAN

When you love
something it
loves you back
in whatever way
it has to love.

JOHN KNOWLES

I HOPE
YOU
REALIZE
HOW
AMAZING
YOU ARE
TO ME

If I could
do nothing
else, I would
daydream
of you.

BALDRIC OF **DOL**

Having you by my side is a gift as we continue to navigate this thing called life.

AMBER LAIGN

LOVE
as hard as
you can, at
all times.

SAM SMITH

Love doesn't cease; love reshapes.

IMAN

I'LL NEVER FORGET THE MOMENT I REALIZED I LOVED YOU

♥

I LOVE YOU

YOU

more than
life itself.

LENA WAITHE

 *I notice you,*
I WANT TO SAY.
EVEN WHEN NO
ONE ELSE DOES,
I DO. I WILL.

DAVID LEVITHAN

You are mine,
and I am yours,
and we are one,
and our lives are
one henceforth.

ROSE CLEVELAND

YOU ARE THE FIRST AND LAST THING ON MY MIND EACH AND EVERY DAY

The richness, beauty and depths of love can only be fully experienced in a climate of complete openness, honesty and vulnerability.

ANTHONY VENN-BROWN

Without warning
as a whirlwind
swoops on an oak.
Love shakes my heart.

SAPPHO

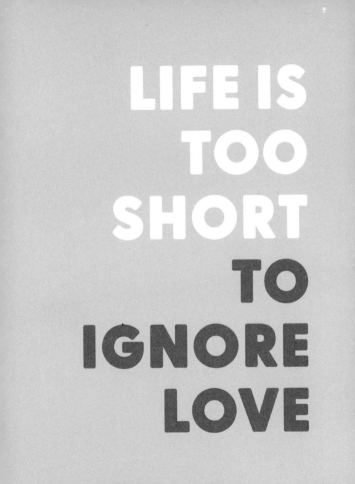

A life without
love is like a year
without summer.

JENNA EVANS WELCH

Nothing is mysterious, no human relation. Except love.

SUSAN SONTAG

LOVE
is friendship
that has
caught fire.

ANN LANDERS

LOVING YOU ISN'T ALWAYS EASY, BUT IT'S ALWAYS WORTH IT

Getting to choose you every day is the best thing.

LAUREN MORELLI

I LIKE IT WHEN YOU SMILE, BUT I LOVE IT WHEN I'M THE REASON

Even in its first
faint traces,
love could alter
a landscape.

ANNA-MARIE McLEMORE

*Who, being loved,
is poor?*

OSCAR WILDE

YOU
MAKE ME
BELIEVE
IN
FOREVER

When everything
within you
and who you're
connecting with
flows... that's love.

OLLY ALEXANDER

Love in all eight tones and all five semitones of the word's full octave.

STEPHEN FRY

YOU'RE THE ONE RISK I'LL ALWAYS TAKE

YOU HAVE
BROKEN DOWN
my defences.
AND I DON'T REALLY
RESENT IT.

VITA SACKVILLE-WEST

Just in case you
ever foolishly
forget; I'm never
not thinking
of you.

VIRGINIA WOOLF

Thus love
has the
magic power
to make of
a beggar
a king.

EMMA GOLDMAN

I KNOW WHAT LOVE IS BECAUSE OF YOU

How lucky I am
to have found what
romance novels call
"my other half".

SANDI TOKSVIG